Chalkboard ART

COLORING BOOK

CJ HUGHES

HAVE AN Awesome DAY

DOVER PUBLICATIONS, INC.
MINEOLA, NEW YORK

D1275175

Usually spotted outside of popular supermarket chains, coffee houses, and book shops, chalk menus have sparked the chalkboard artist's recent rise in popularity. In this latest edition to Dover's *Creative Haven* series for the experienced colorist, thirty-one ready-to-color illustrations feature the hand-drawn lettering and carefully rendered illustrations reminiscent of chalkboard art around the world. The detailed illustrations are perfect for experimentation with color technique, and the perforated, unbacked pages make displaying your finished work easy.

Chloe Clem

Bibliographical Note

Chalkboard Art Coloring Book is a new work,
first published by Dover Publications, Inc., in 2015.

International Standard Book Number

ISBN-13: 978-0-486-80210-7
ISBN-10: 0-486-80210-8

Manufactured in the United States by RR Donnelley
80210802   2015
www.doverpublications.com

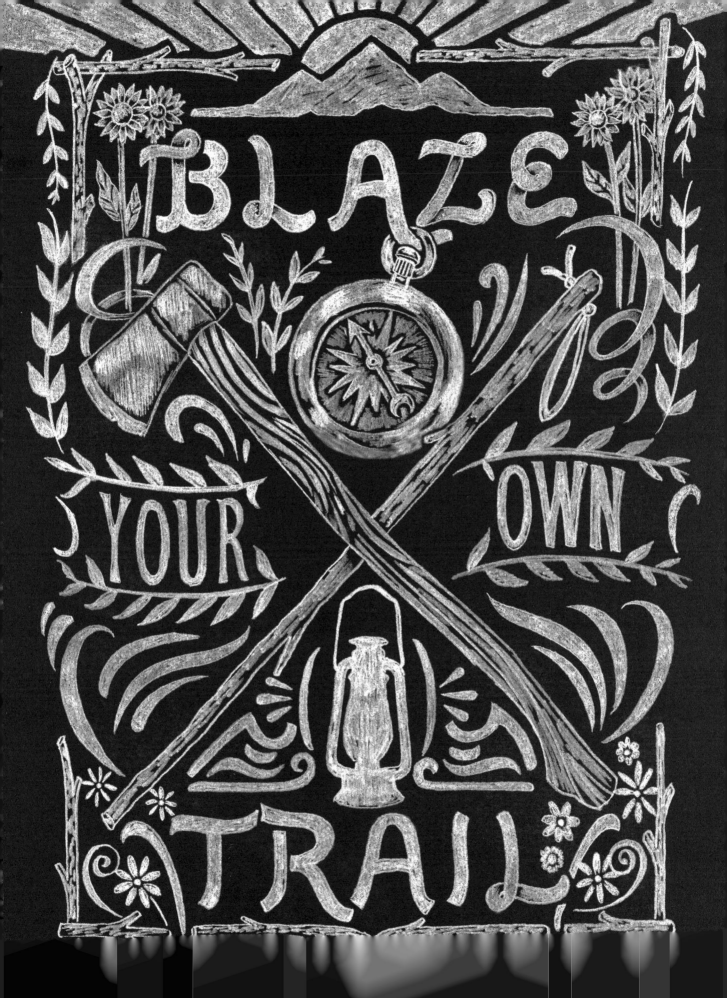

FIND BEAUTY IN THE ordinary

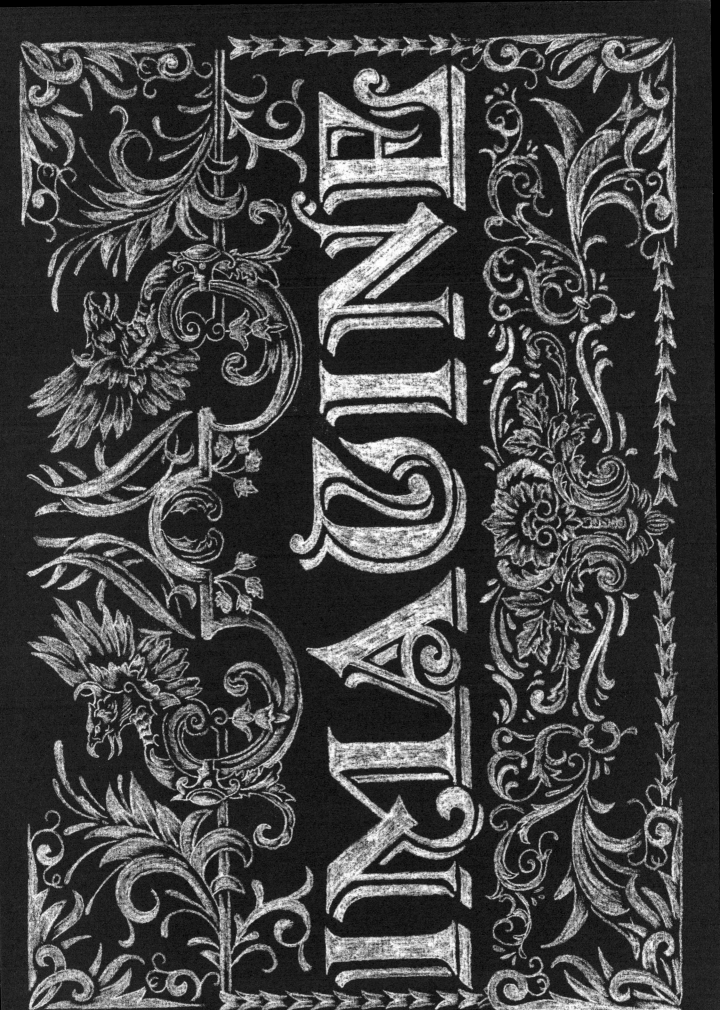

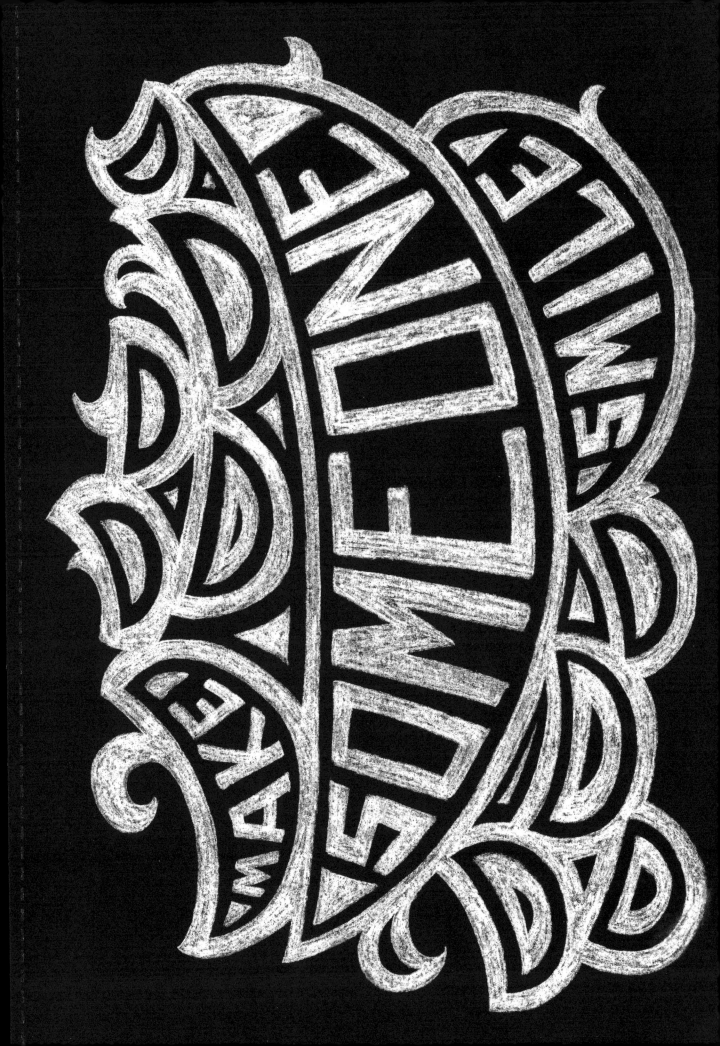